5000 Miles to India

Madan Gopal Bali

1967

BlueRose Publishers
NewDelhi • London

First Published in August 2021

ISBN: 978-93-5472-303-2

BLUEROSE PUBLISHERS

www.bluerosepublishers.com

info@bluerosepublishers.com

+91 8882 898 898

Cover Design:

Swati Singh

Typographic Design:

Tanya Raj Upadhyay

Distributed by: BlueRose, Amazon, Flipkart

It is not only the destination,
but the journey that makes your experience
wholesome and complete...

\- ***M.G.Bali***

In loving memory of Late Shri Madan Gopal Bali (Author) from his wife and all children, on his 86th Birthday - 8th August, 2021.

"WE LIVE IN YOUR LOVE !"

INTRODUCTION

Late fifties and the sixties were an exciting time to be in England. It was the time of Beatles (music Band) making a worldwide mark, England making a dramatic economic recovery after the second world war and youth getting good employment, England winning the football world cup in1966. It was during this exciting time that my father got the opportunity to study engineering at the *Lanchester College of Technology, Coventry.*

After arriving in England (in1956) by sea, he got immersed in the exciting environment in UK. In addition to finishing his engineering and working for *General Electric Company* in Coventry, he boosted his multi-talented personality by pursuing his royal tastes in art, music, sports, and flying (WW-I Tiger Moth planes). In the year 1967, he decided to go back to India. However, the adventurer in him soon took control of his actions and he decided to drive all the way to his native place Daryabad in U.P., India in his VW Beetle car.

Intercontinental travelling by road in the sixties, had a different set of challenges than today. The good thing was that there were no active wars taking place en-route to India.

On the downside there were no GPS, or mobiles. The presence of lights, hotels or petrol pumps, on the highways was bare minimum. To top it all, the names of the places seen on the map were at times, different altogether. Europe was not as integrated as it is now, and one had to have visa for each and every country one passes through, and get the currency converted to the local currency. Coupled with this, one would not always find a tar road to drive. Most of Europe had cobbled road and many places in Asia had no road or roads that were hard to find, especially in the desert areas. Tackling well-armed nomadic tribes or wild animals en-route was the scariest challenge.

As they say, "well begun is half done" so my father did meticulous planning to embark on his journey of a lifetime. He did extensive research for this epic travel. He also communicated with Volkswagen and an organization called *The Automobile Club*, from where he got a huge set of data. They sent him detailed reports of the different routes he could take for his journey. Logs of places between two cities and distances, along with maps and the kind of road he would encounter at each place. It is astounding to see the detailed bulk of information he received from them, which proved to be pillars of guiding light for him.

As per the entries in his passport, this travel started on 15th Feb,1967, and ended on 15th April'1967. A full two months of pure adventure!

Though he was an excellent writer, as you will see further, but getting him to write was a task. He always wanted to pen down this travelogue but couldn't find the time and peace of mind to do so.

Finally, it came in ink only when he decided to work no more, in the year 2004-05.

When in 2005 he suddenly passed away, leaving the family in complete shock, the digitization of this work was still incomplete. Later, on taking a break from job, I started compiling this Travelogue, and my two brothers and sister helped me in giving final shape to this dream project, and making it ready for the publishers. I also thank all friends and family who motivated me in this endeavour.

My father's journey was mighty challenging, risky and required a great deal of mental and emotional strength to survive, and take on new situations at each step. Everyone has their own fears, but the one who faces it head on with intelligence and wits, is the winner.

Hope you have a great time reading about this historic travel, and it inspires you to embark upon a journey of your own.

The Travel Route

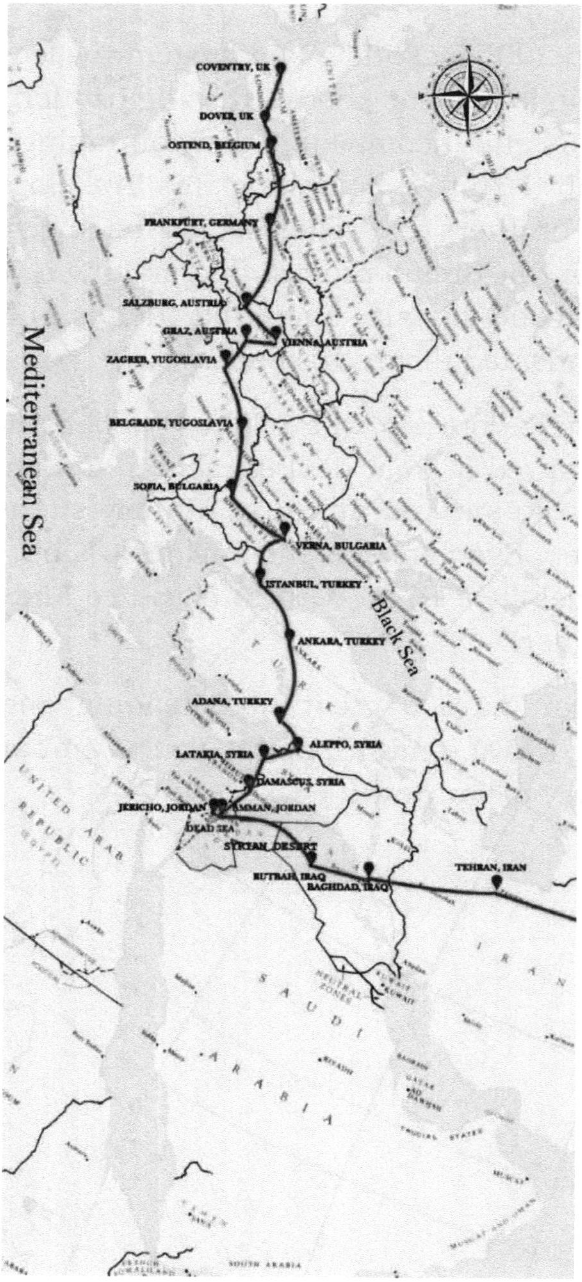

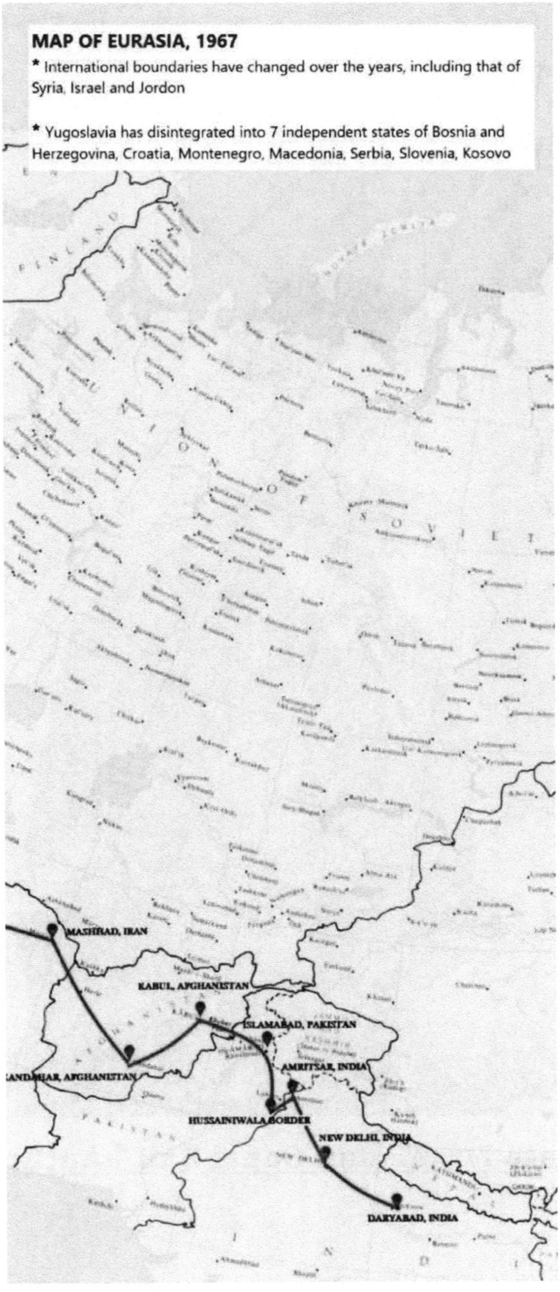

Map prepared by Mrs. Radhika Bali Sarup (daughter)

Late Mr. Madan Gopal Bali - Author

ABOUT THE AUTHOR

When you think of a person like my father, his magnetic aura fills your heart. People like him are rare - benevolent, quiet, humble, loving unconditionally, throwing an enigmatic and affectionate smile. Their smile speaks more than words and eyes radiate a divine sparkle. When you meet them, they don't seek attention, but draw your attention to themselves by extraordinary deeds of their genius minds. That was him - kind and honest, truthful to the core and very soft spoken, his disposition would always say -

"***I have nothing to declare but my genius***..."

Prestigious Family History –

Near the historic city of Lucknow in Uttar Pradesh, India, is another important town named Daryabad. About a century ago, it was called the Rampur-Daryabad State. "Bali Family" is a distinguished Taluqdar (Land-Owners) family of Daryabad, which was running that state since generations. My grandfather, Dr. Rai Rajeshwar Bali, was the Taluqdar of Rampur-Daryabad State, a prominent political figure, a reformist and a connoisseur of Music and art of his time. He was addressed as "Raja Saheb" and was very well respected for his noble heart and pioneering works. As the Health & Education minister of the Local Self Government of the United Province (now Uttar Pradesh), he was rapidly transforming the Education pattern and policies of the government.

He established the very reputed Bhatkhande Music College, Lucknow, which streamlined Hindustani music in a single uniform model. He also set the stone for Primary Education Act, Secondary Education Boards, Agra University Act and Lucknow Art Gallery. For the first time, he introduced music and dance as regular subjects in colleges, un- caging it from its confinement in brothels and bringing it out front stage to the educated class. His health reforms are still a proud mark in history, and well acclaimed by the then Governor, Sir William Marris in his testimonial. Prominent leaders of India, like Pt. Govind Vallabh Pant, Dr. Radhakrishnan and the likes were fascinated by his remarkable work. He played an important role in the protest against the historic *Simon Commission* in the year 1928, successfully voted it out in the Legislative Assembly, but subsequently resigned as being a minister he was in strong disagreement to the policies of the British government.

But that was not all, apart from being a great administrator and reformist, my grandfather was also a profound Krishna devotee by heart. The day he left politics, he came home, took off his *sherwani* (as if renouncing that role) and immersed himself in Krishna Devotion by writing verses on Him. Such was his dynamic and magnificent personality.

He enthralled his passion for music, art, theatre and philosophy to his family by making a library in the compound of family's residential premises, called "Deorhi". The library housed very rare books on Indian and Chinese Art. Original paintings of legendary artists, books of Indian and western philosophers, history of the world and many more. My father, the author of this Travelogue, grew up in this sea of knowledge. He had a comfortable sofa in the library where he would spend hours reading, day in and day out.

His mother, Mrs Sheela Bali, was from Sialkot, Punjab – a strong, educated, knowledgeable and extremely talented woman. She complimented her husband, my grandfather equally well, and was a huge source of inspiration for my father. Her art works mostly hand embroidered on cloth, adorned the huge hallways of the palace. She was an exceptionally talented singer of Indian Classical music, and completed writing a rare compilation of briefs of all characters from the stories of *Puranas* in Hindi, in alphabetical order.

Rai Rajeshwar Bali & Smt. Sheela Bali (father & mother)

"Deorhi" had a huge compound like a fort, a big gate, a temple and many big palace- like buildings in which each family lived. The state had a small army of its own, including elephants and horses.

Author's home in Daryabad, Deorhi

Bali family was at the epitome of a rich culture. All festivals were celebrated with oodles of music, art, decorations and sumptuous food, including sweet delicacies. Huge sets were erected on occasions to host a play related to the festivals like Janmashtmi and Ram Navami. Members of the family would act in them, while my grandfather wrote those epic plays, all a masterpiece of Hindi literature. Renowned artist, Asit Kumar Haldar from Shanti Niketan and reputed local artist, Mirza Sahib were invited to design the sets. My father's uncle Sri S.N. Bali was a talented music composer in All India Radio, who used to give music to all the songs of the play. Though I never got to see those plays, but listening to their descriptions fills my heart with colours.

However, after the early demise of Dr. Rai Rajeshwar Bali in 1944, things changed drastically, and owing to some issues of distant family members, who wanted everything to themselves, led to a lot of trouble. Thankfully my father's siblings and their first cousins had a very strong bond between them.

AUTHOR'S PERSONA -

The legacy and the environment he got, gave wings to all his talents, and inculcated the foundation of a great character. Born on 8th August,1935, he was the fourth out of five sons (and three daughters) of such a legendary father. Hence, most of his childhood was princely, leisurely and enjoyable. He finished his schooling from Colvin Taluqdar's College, Lucknow. In those times, students of reputed families had the luxury of having a personal servant with them in the hostel. He was a brilliant student, but a mischievous one too. He left an indelible impression not only on his teachers, principal, school mates, but also on the walls and ceilings of the school.

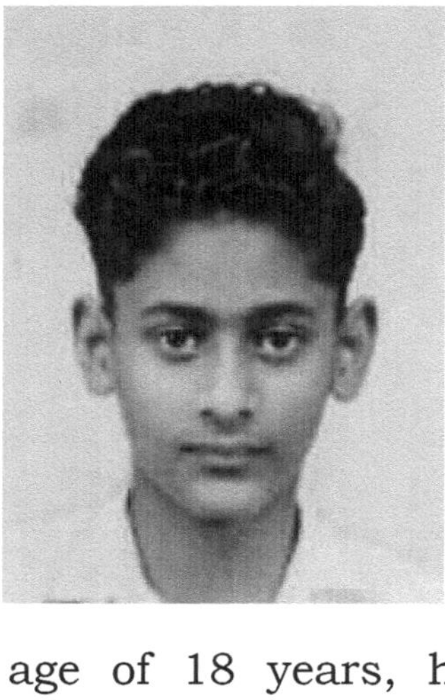

At the young age of 18 years, he developed a telephone and an Intercom all by himself. This amazed everyone and brought his genius to the forefront. All family members who came to know about this, insisted on his getting into engineering. However, he got permission from his mother only when he promised that he would come back as a bachelor to marry the girl of her choice only. She couldn't stand the thought of a cross -cultural daughter-in-law. His love and fondness for his mother and a strong character made him keep up with this promise. About two years later, in the year 1957, my eldest Uncle, Late Rai Dinanath Bali sent him to England to pursue Engineering. He travelled there by sea, a journey he relished very often.

Owing to his comfortable upbringing, managing on his own was difficult in the beginning. He shared, "I used to get teary eyed when I felt thirsty, there was no one to give me water." Gradually he got a grip on his new life in England, where he had come to fulfil his dreams, and in no time, was on top of things. He worked really hard to not only complete all his chores, but also sustain himself. Being a diligent person, he attended office during the day, and night school in the evening to pursue his studies.

His unique habit of a 7-minute nap to refresh his mind was a saving grace. Studying in advance, what was going to be taught next in class was also a habit that made him grasp concepts easily and permanently. Weekends were spent on cricket, chess, organizing Indian and Western Classical music concerts, and sometimes parties.

Music was his passion. He owned the Hi-Fi AKAI Music system, and a rare collection of classics of his time. He sincerely believed that all hearts could be won with music on your side. That is how he won many celebrity friends as well. His prized possession of music came all the way to India and gave us beautiful melodies as well as memories.

In addition to all this, he joined the flying club. What made him venture into flying an aircraft is still a mystery to me, as he had fear of heights. Moreover, the only vehicle he had driven till now was a bicycle. He narrated his experience about his very first flight to us, and shared that when the plane took off and started ascending in the skies for the first time, panic gripped him badly. He started shaking and perspiring, and was on the verge of losing control, but held on strongly. In a few minutes, his heart started feeling light and cool, and he found himself enjoying the aerial view. From then on, there was no looking back, he had triumphed his greatest fear, and he could fly even before he learnt to drive a car.

<u>Flying WW-1, Tiger Moth plane</u>

Later on, he realised that car driving could further improve his flying skills, so he bought a car and learnt driving too. In those days, clearing the driving test for getting a License was very tough in England. People took two to three attempts to pass it, but not him. His sharp learning skills earned a pat from the instructor, who was still in disbelief.

The innate qualities that came from his family in him and all his siblings, who were all gems in their own way, were obviously art, music, poetry and philosophy. My mother, Mrs. VijayBala Bali also possesses great talent in music and shared common interests in all these arts. She became his advisor and best critic in all his artistic and literary endeavours.

He had learnt sketching from the renowned artist of his time, Asit Kumar Haldar. However, the mischievous shade of his own character made him draw cartoons too. This hobby made him very popular wherever he went, when he would bring out the funny face of people around him, including himself. While penning this travelogue, he had made sketches of his car and friends he met on the way.

Mr. Bali's cartoon of himself

After returning to India, he never boasted about his exceptional achievements, but made sure to pass on the wisdom of his experiences to his four children, and to friends and family who sought it from him, unconditionally. Being an introvert, he never sought attention consciously. However, his enigmatic personality and calm aura drew people to him, who were in awe of his accomplishments.

Since childhood, I listened to most of his adventure stories, but never realised their gravity. It was only when I started compiling this Travelogue written by him, that his whole persona dawned upon me. Suddenly I had so many revelations about him, and I couldn't imagine what a passionate, courageous, daring and popular person he was. Hence working on his Travelogue proved to be my own journey of knowing him completely.

I wish he would have written this Travelogue much earlier!

His real - life stories and anecdotes of this epic travel, spread immense pleasure and pride in our family that will always be treasured. We consider it an honour and a privilege to pass on his legacy through this Travelogue.

- Mrs. Devika Bali Mathur

PREFACE

I have a cousin, who, if he decides to walk across a field that is almost the size of a football field, that has a one-inch-wide covered drain going through it, which happens to have just one brick missing, his foot is sure to land into the hole, bang on target.

I, for once, am not accident prone but I do seem to attract some bizarre, funny or awkward situations to cope with at every turn and corner of my progress in the journey.

Therefore, this travelogue is more of a collection of these anecdotes deeply imprinted in my memory, rather than a host of famous sights I saw, which have become quite hazy over the span of forty years. As soon as I came back to India, I got married to a lovely girl and with a brood of four children and their bringing up, kept me utterly busy. I had no time to write anything. Now that I have reached the tender age of 70 years, I am in my semi-retirement mode; I have attempted to narrate this quite unusual story now.

I can feel the youthful hot-blooded zeal for attempting such a trip. Men like Sir Francis Cheshester who single handedly sailed a dingy small boat across the Atlantic, from America to England.

Charles Lindsburg, who flew a small plane across the Atlantic to Paris and Sir Donald Campbell were truly great, for they were pioneers, breaking new grounds and raising the thresholds. They were my heroes. They had fired my young mind on this path of adventure. In comparison, my attempt was merely a minimum attempt and that too on a beaten track.

I did prepare my car thoroughly, which was a saving grace. My car was of the right kind and the modifications proved their worth. Food, petrol, clothing etc. were okay. It was only my training and upbringing which was somewhat royal, that made it very tough indeed. In the heart of the desert that spread over 700 miles, in my utter loneliness and bitterness, I often used to curse myself for landing myself in this hell.

Living a nomadic life where my car had become my house and a flimsy shelter against nature and other dangers. Sometimes going hungry, sometimes making soups from packets and dipping well stacked bread slices and gulping them down. I had tinned meat, fish and cheese which was merely rolled into a slice of bread. If the tinned stuff was short in supply, some mango or mixed pickle filled the gap between the slices. In towns big or small, “seekh kababs” and “naans” were available. It all makes my mouth water now, but eating those, day in and day out, their mere sight was nauseating. All one craved for was home cooked food, no matter of what kind.

Living the life of a gypsy – a vagabond kind of existence for months together was no joke for me.

However painful it was, it was definitely the greatest experience of my life. *In the process of growing into an evolved human being, this pilgrimage was immeasurably valuable. This is where one completely loses one's identity. I was no longer an engineer, a royal, an artist etc.- just a consciousness experiencing the various facets of the journey of life. This was a truly humbling lesson in itself.* Imagine yourself waking up in the morning in your car- you see a street dog you think and say, 'Hello! My friend! You and I are sailing in the same boat! We do not know what to expect or what is in store for us by the end of the day.' He wagged his tail and I gave him 2 slices of bread. He looked mighty pleased and wagged his tail again. I dared not give him more, you never know you may run short of bread and would be doomed. These kinds of situations were the everyday harsh realities that one faces.

I came close and direct with people ranging from hardcore criminals to the most decent and simple ones, ordinary lovable people of many races and classes. I discovered that no matter what the color, race or creed they belonged to, fundamentally, they were all the same. Good, Bad, Wicked, ill-tempered or even violent, they shared something in common, a soft and human corner in their heart. If one is able to touch that part, they change, bend, become extremely helpful and friendly.

This insight into human behaviour is priceless. A charming smile, soft and friendly behaviour and simple talk on your part can melt most hearts. This attitude and perception had led me through innumerable piquant situations.

\-

Madan Gopal Bali

EVENT SUMMARY

CHAPTER-1

BIRTH AND BUILD UP OF MY ADVENTUROUS ZEAL

In the winters of 1966, I was enjoying the company of friends in a Pub of Coventry in England. I had become a full-fledged Electronics Engineer and had been working for G.E.C. for the last five years or so and pressure was now building up from home to return to India, especially from my mother. I knew her main concern was that it was dangerous to leave an eligible bachelor in the glittering and alluring world of damsels in England. I was about to finalize the date of departure when an idea crossed my mind. We had a G.E.C. flying club of which I was a member and was receiving training for P.P.L. (Private Pilots License) - why not go to India on a small plane? Just then, somebody mentioned an advertisement in the newspaper that an old Tiger Moth was for sale for ₤400/= which was in those days, cheaper than a car. I rushed to the address but my plans were shattered when I learnt that the hangarage and the upkeep of the plane would run into over a thousand pounds per year, which was rather, too costly a venture. The next viable alternative was going to India over land by car. This idea grew on me and soon became an obsession. No maps were easily available so the Readers Digest Atlas came in quite handy for the initial planning.

My elder brother Kailash Nath Bali Bhaisahib was in Kenya those days and my first priority was to go to Kenya and from there take a ship to Bombay and then drive down to Lucknow. That would mean going up to Aqaba and driving through Egypt and going along the extremely hazardous road along the

Nile through Sudan. But Sudan was having trouble with neighbors and not issuing visas; as a result, this route had to be abandoned. Now the last route available was to cross Europe and enter Turkey through Syria, Jordan, Iraq, Iran, Afghanistan and Pakistan to India. Broadly, the route was final and the process of obtaining the visas etc. and writing to all the Embassies got going but choosing the right kind of car and the companion was yet to be decided.

There was a wonderful Organization called the *Consumers Association* which reviewed in its monthly magazine the performance of consumer items. Fortunately, they had reviewed mid-priced cars of all makers that were available in U.K. This made my choice of car infinitely easier. I needed a robust car, which would be able to cope with the very tough roads and desert conditions. It should have minimum minor and major break down rate. It should also have its own service centers en-route where its spares were easily available.

German Volkswagen (VW) Beetle footed the bill admirably. It had in addition the advantage of having an air-cooled engine – a boon in the desert. Promptly, with the help of my friend Len Venus, a very good, couple of months old, second hand Volkswagen was purchased. Volkswagen was gaining admiration by the consumers in England and quite a lot of VW Beetles were to be seen on the roads. Their owners seemed to belong to a fraternity of their own. Soon I was contacted by a gentleman called Tom Clark who was an avid fan of VW's. His garage had a ramp and all the tools that one could think of.

I had written to the Volkswagen people about my proposed trip. They had suggested that I fit a guard to protect the square pipe welded to the body of the jack and also a grill shield and a steel channel to protect the aluminum engine. These simple protections proved their worth.

My friend Tom Clarke gave a queer suggestion which was difficult to digest. The VW's engine was located under the chassis behind the back seat. The clutch, accelerator levers were therefore connected to the foot pedals through cables. They could snap at the joints. To change the cables, required difficult maneuvers, considerable time and effort. So, he suggested that I cut a rectangular hole 1.5 x 1.00 ft. in the chassis floor right on top of the engine. How could I allow such a big hole to be cut in my dear car? I protested vehemently. He took me to his car which looked like a brand-new VW, gleaming red with a small oval glass window at the back with the latest 1500 cc embossed on it. I was shocked to learn that it was in fact the original ancient model produced during Hitler's reign. Tom had taken care to update it every time VW introduced a modification in the body or the engine with their newer models. Now the rear window and the side windows were much larger and the engine was more powerful. I was amazed to find that he had done it all in this very garage-cum workshop.

Now I needed no persuasion. Tom carefully marked a portion to be removed with a piece of chalk and set – squares and after making a number of holes, he cut a small portion to accommodate a pair of scissors which had a three inch blade and four feet long handles. With this strange contraption, he deftly cut the rectangular hole with nice rounded corners. Another sheet was cut to size and made to cover this hole. A small steel-wire was nicely tucked beside it.

The hole was an excellent idea and possibly saved my life once when the clutch cable broke and I was passing through the most dangerous part of Turkey. I merely opened the cover and tied the wire to the clutch lever using my left hand to operate it. This way I covered the remaining 70-80 miles to Ankara to spend the night safely, and got a new cable installed in the morning. On reaching India, I had a closer look and was shocked to find that both these protections had received a severe beating and without them I would have been in serious trouble. Punctures often took place on those rough roads, and without the guard and the grill, the square pipe that held the jack to lift the car, would have definitely broken. They were already damaged at many places by stones.

By now, this venture was no longer a secret. The word soon got around that a loony Indian was preparing an overland trip to India. People started pouring in to help me which was encouraging and gave me confidence and helped me choose a companion, Eric Simpson, a robust Englishman, who was gentle but tough and with whom I could get along nicely.

One more gentleman who visited me gave me the most valuable advice for desert travel. He was a member of the rescue squad in the British Army during the war in the Desert. According to him there were a few cardinal rules for the Army in the desert. The first was to carry abundant quantities of water and petrol. Even if you have a small Vaseline bottle, either fill it with water or petrol and carry it with you. One should only stop at big towns but while on the road, keep moving and don't stop unless you are forced to. Most of the nomads lurking in the desert were armed and potentially very dangerous. He was so fastidious on this point that he brought a stop watch and made me practice changing the stepney wheel within 4-5 minutes. He also showed me how to extract water from the desert sand, a spoonful, enough for survival. Finally, he told me that in case I thought I was really lost and could not find my way, don't panic and start searching the way. This was a waste of a lot of energy. Instead I should stay put and soon someone would find me. This I found was true, but is easier said than done for only a maha-yogi can detach himself to a state of immobility in a situation like that.

We then intensified our efforts to obtain the visas, maps and the Carnet- an international document for the car which exempts it from import- export formalities in transit. The first shock came when we were told that owing to strained relations with India, Pakistan was not issuing visas to Indians. This was quite disturbing and a stumbling block. By now, I was in touch with the *Royal Automobile Club (RAC*) and the *Automobile Association (AA*) who gave a wealth of information, including maps.

In order to by-pass Pakistan, an alternative was to take a boat from Khurman Shahar, a port in the Persian Gulf to Bombay. But it was not certain whether I would be able to take my car with me. However, we decided to risk it and go ahead with our plan.

One evening while Eric and I were discussing the remaining details in the pub, news came that a party of English Boys were robbed somewhere in the Middle East and they took away all their belongings, including the clothes they were wearing. They had to walk 50 odd miles to their Embassy-naked. That was a shocking revelation and I could see poor Eric was badly shaken. There was a general antagonism against the British in the Arab world in those days. As a result, Eric opted out of this trip.

It was a shattering blow for me. At this stage it was not possible to find another partner to complete the necessary formalities which would delay the trip by a few months. Now, my choice was limited to either going all alone or giving up the plan altogether.

As I said earlier, the plan had grown on me and had become an obsession. My young blood refused to hold back and give up the plan and accept defeat.

Besides, I had already put in at least 7-8 months acquiring all the visas and other documents. I could discern a distinct change in the attitude of people around me. The venture they generally thought, was a little crazy. Doing it alone was downright loony, especially so with the adverse stories trickling in. Even now, I marvel at how I gathered so much courage against such odds.

Another compelling factor was the recent epic crossing of the Atlantic Ocean by Francis Chichester in a small boat all alone. I would follow his progress with baited breath on the Radio and TV. About the same time, I read the biography of Charles Lindberg, describing his Epic maiden flight in a single seater plane 'Kitty Hawk' from America to Paris. He had fitted extra-large tanks to accommodate extra fuel he needed and his plane barely managed to lift off the ground.

At about the same time, I had also seen Donald Campbell break his land speed record on his jet-propelled boat '*Blue Bird*' at Salt Lake, Australia for the first time T.V. link up. Just before he started, he was asked if he was afraid. He said, ***'Only a mad man would jump blindly into a dangerous mission without fear. He could overcome his fear to some extent by thoroughly going over what could go wrong and preparing himself for such an eventuality.'***

As luck would have it, on his way back, a choppy wave smashed through his boat and he perished with it. My heart sank, but his last words kept ringing in my ears. I salute him for his brave and great effort.

They had become my heroes and fired my imagination. They were truly great for they were pioneers who crossed the frontiers of human endeavor. My effort would at best be a humble effort and that too on a beaten track. Hence, the die was cast. I started packing my belongings, which was quite a task. I was going to leave the country which had become my second home in a span of more than a decade, and a third of my life to date. Finally, I was going on my own, and the date for departure was fixed for 15th February, 1967.

After a series of farewell parties, I slipped away quietly, early in the morning to avoid any emotional scenes. Cruising along the MI Motorway, I noticed that as the car heaved up and down, sometimes the tires touched the mud –guards. It was definitely overloaded. In London I left my AKAI tape recorder with a friend to be sent later and dumped heavy articles into dustbins of side streets shedding more than 80 kgs. of baggage.

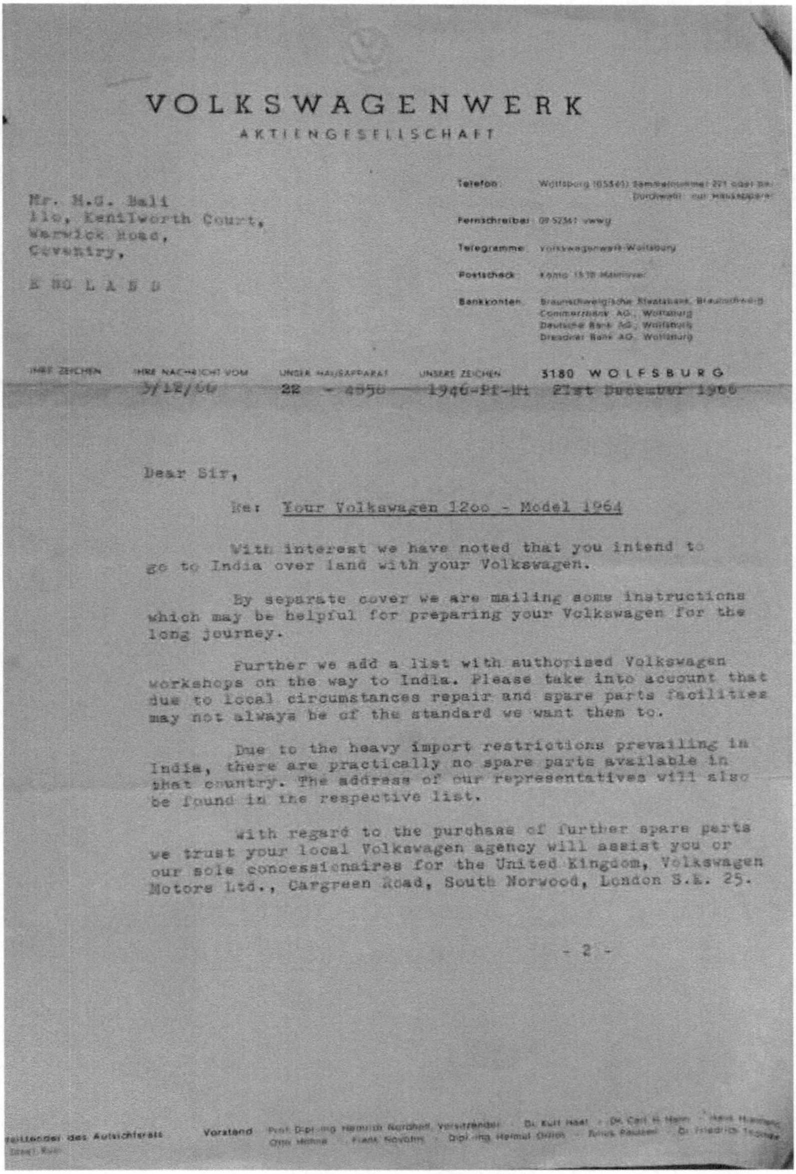

VOLKSWAGENWERK

AKTIENGESELLSCHAFT

Telefon: Wolfsburg (05361) Sammelnummer 271 oder bei Durchwahl zur Hausapparat

Fernschreiber: 09 52341 vwwg

Telegramme: Volkswagenwerk Wolfsburg

Postscheck: Konto 1510 Hannover

Bankkonten: Braunschweigische Staatsbank, Braunschweig; Commerzbank AG., Wolfsburg; Deutsche Bank AG., Wolfsburg; Dresdner Bank AG., Wolfsburg

Mr. H.G. Bali
11o, Kenilworth Court,
Warwick Road,
Coventry,

E N G L A N D

IHRE ZEICHEN	IHRE NACHRICHT VOM	UNSER HAUSAPPARAT	UNSERE ZEICHEN	3180 WOLFSBURG
	3/12/66	22 - 2558	1946-PI-Hi	21st December 1966

Dear Sir,

Re: Your Volkswagen 12oo - Model 1964

With interest we have noted that you intend to go to India over land with your Volkswagen.

By separate cover we are mailing some instructions which may be helpful for preparing your Volkswagen for the long journey.

Further we add a list with authorised Volkswagen workshops on the way to India. Please take into account that due to local circumstances repair and spare parts facilities may not always be of the standard we want them to.

Due to the heavy import restrictions prevailing in India, there are practically no spare parts available in that country. The address of our representatives will also be found in the respective list.

With regard to the purchase of further spare parts we trust your local Volkswagen agency will assist you or our sole concessionaires for the United Kingdom, Volkswagen Motors Ltd., Cargreen Road, South Norwood, London S.E. 25.

\- 2 -

Vorsitzender des Aufsichtsrats ... Vorstand: Prof. Dipl.-Ing. Heinrich Nordhoff, Vorsitzender · Dr. Kurt Hael · Dr. Carl H. Hahn · Hans Hiemenz · Otto Höhne · Frank Novotny · Dipl.-Ing. Helmut Orlich · Julius Paulsen · Dr. Friedrich Thomée

Letter from VW

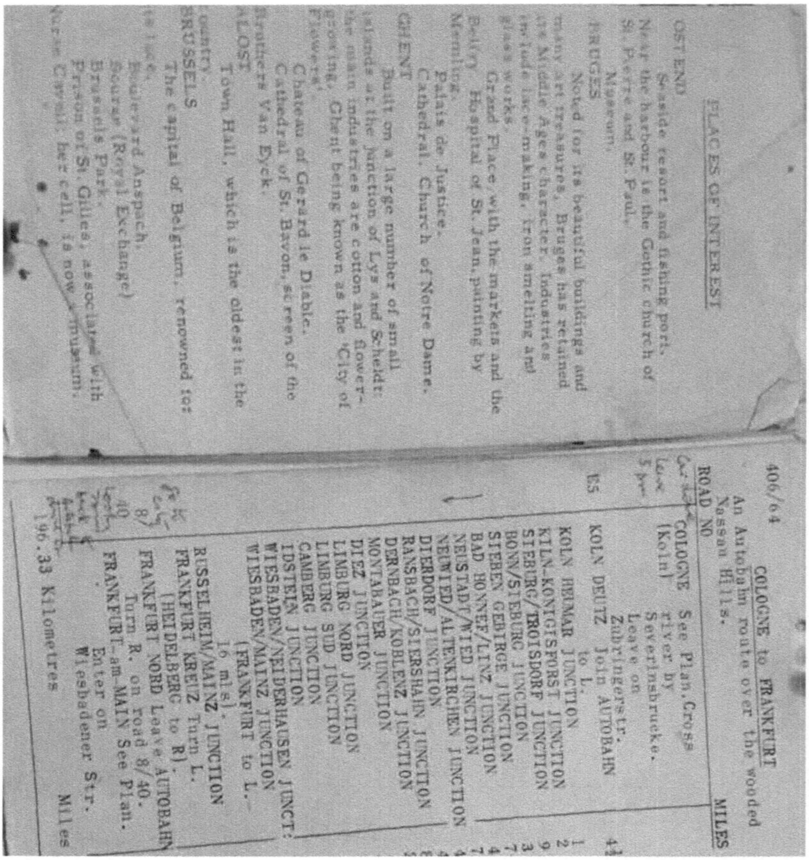

PLACES OF INTEREST

OSTEND
Seaside resort and fishing port. Near the harbour is the Gothic church of St. Pierre and St. Paul.
Museum.

BRUGES
Noted for its beautiful buildings and many art treasures, Bruges has retained its Middle Ages character. Industries include lace-making, iron smelting and glass works.
Grand Place, with the markets and the Belfry. Hospital of St. Jean, painting by Memling.
Palais de Justice.
Cathedral. Church of Notre Dame.

GHENT
Built on a large number of small islands at the junction of Lys and Scheldt: the main industries are cotton and flower-growing, Ghent being known as the 'City of Flowers'.
Chateau of Gerard le Diable.
Cathedral of St. Bavon, screen of the Brothers Van Eyck.

ALOST
Town Hall, which is the oldest in the country.

BRUSSELS
The capital of Belgium, renowned for its lace.
Boulevard Anspach.
Bourse (Royal Exchange)
Brussels Park.
Prison of St. Gilles, associated with Nurse Cavell; her cell, is now a museum.

406/64

COLOGNE to FRANKFURT

An Autobahn route over the wooded Nassau Hills.

ROAD NO — MILES

COLOGNE (Koln) See Plan. Cross river by Severinsbrucke. Leave on Zubringerstr.
E5 KOLN DEUTZ Join AUTOBAHN to L. 4½
KOLN HEUMAR JUNCTION
KILN-KONIGISFORST JUNCTION
SIEBURG/TROISDORF JUNCTION
BONN/SIEBURG JUNCTION
SIEBEN GEBIRGE JUNCTION
BAD HONNEF/LINZ JUNCTION
NEUSTADT/WIED JUNCTION
NEUWIED/ALTENKIRCHEN JUNCTION
DIERDORF JUNCTION
RANSBACH/SIERSHAHN JUNCTION
DERNBACH/KOBLENZ JUNCTION
MONTABAUER JUNCTION
DIEZ JUNCTION
LIMBURG NORD JUNCTION
LIMBURG SUD JUNCTION
CAMBERG JUNCTION
IDSTEIN JUNCTION
WIESBADEN/NEIDERHAUSEN JUNCT:
WIESBADEN/MAINZ JUNCTION (FRANKFURT to L. - 16 mls).
RUSSELHEIM/MAINZ JUNCTION
FRANKFURT KREUZ Turn L. (HEIDELBERG to R).
FRANKFURT NORD Leave AUTOBAHN Turn R. on road 8/40.
FRANKFURT-am-MAIN See Plan. Enter on Wiesbadener Str.
196.33 Kilometres — Miles

Detailed Log of places en- route provided by The Royal Automobile Club

CHAPTER – 2

BON VOYAGE - ADIEU ENGLAND, MY SECOND HOME

Next day I was on my way to Dover from where the car was loaded on a ferry to cross the English Channel. On the decks of the ferry, the coast - line of England receded, leaving behind memories of all the wonderful times I had in England, that I had come to love so dearly and was in tears. That sight of leaving behind my second home has been embedded in my memory forever.

The Sea was fairly calm and a few hours of smooth sailing landed us at Ostend in Belgium. As I drove the car through the Gangway, I was surprised to find that I had come on a cobbled road. It was a delightful experience. In those days, quite a part of Ostend had cobbled surface, which gave a tremendous continental feel.

GERMANY- The fatherland of my Car

Next morning, I was on German soil, the fatherland of my VW. I thought it would be wiser to get it checked and serviced for she was unlikely to receive a better treatment after leaving Germany. So, I took her to a large VW garage and explained that I was taking her to India for good and just to see if she needs a minor tonic.

The proprietor asked me to return after 45 minutes. I loitered around and was back in an hour. I was shocked to find that he had prepared an estimate of Pounds 16 flat. A little argument and he took me inside. I was aghast to find all the engine parts, piston, valves and the lot neatly laid out on a table and the body of the car hanging 20 feet above the ground. I had no choice but to get the job done. He asked me to come after an hour.

In those days England had imposed a maximum limit of Pounds 50.00 that one could carry out of the country. My main worry was parting with a third of it before entering the thick and thin of my journey. So, I offered to give him a cheque which he gladly accepted and saved the situation.

Within the hour, the car had been assembled and undergone final checks. The new bounce delighted me and she was as good as new. Later, it never had any problems for the next One Lac miles (1,60,000 Kms). Hats off to German thoroughness and technical excellence.

***Lovely Austria* -**

To save expenses, the strategy was to spend minimal time in the continent. Therefore, without wasting any time I moved on. By the evening I was over the borders of Austria. Now, I was in the continent and had to change over to the right side of the road, which was getting on my nerves. Hence, I decided to cross the border and rest in a hotel at night. As it was off – season, I could manage a room for 10 Shillings for the night which was not too bad. A hearty meal, a good night's rest in a cozy bed and a lovely breakfast was all one could have wished for.

Rolling along the Austrian countryside, I saw the very places where 'The Sound of Music' was shot. One felt as if, any moment, Julie Andrews would stumble out of the lush green hills and meadows and fill the scene with her sound of music.

Negotiating this part of the Alps was not easy in the evening. The mountainous winding road was devoid of any traffic. Still, sometimes a reddish light flashed across the rear window which intrigued me. Though I do not believe in ghosts, the flashing of lights was ghostly. Finally, I was much relieved to arrive at the border post. There was a raised embankment with a 'stop' sign on the lamp post on my right. The moment I put my foot down to stop the car, there was a loud clanging of metal at the rear coupled with a severe jolt. I jumped out of my car to find a man meekly peeping out of a queer looking car. A sharp altercation followed but the tension eased a little on finding that there was only a minor damage to the bumper fitting.

Apparently, his lights had failed and it was pitch dark. He had therefore hitched himself to my tail lights and expertly followed me over the serpentine roads through the Alps; the red flashes of light on my rear window were no more than the reflection of my tail lights on the chrome parts of his car.

Though the sound of the collision had reverberated throughout the valley, there was another welcoming feature. He was a Dutch man and could speak reasonably good English. So many days had passed communicating mostly in sign language; I was dying to be able to speak to someone. He also seemed to like me and we had a hearty chat, I don't know for how long? We decided to go ahead to Sofia to fill our empty tummies. So that is how we virtually bumped into each other – bumper to bumper so to speak.

Like the owner, even the car was a strange version of Citroen. Outwardly, no regard was paid to its appearance. The inside had no frills; it was simply covered with pieces of hardboard. A lever, with the appearance like that of a walking stick, sprouted out of the front dashboard and was actually its gear system. It was fun to watch him frantically push, pull and twist this 'walking stick' every time he changed gears. But mind you- she was tough like him. Its utility on a journey like this was invaluable. The two seats were moored to the chassis floor by a set of hooks. Needing no tools, the seats could be taken out and put on the ground to enjoy the scenery. Once the seats were out, the car turned into a spacious bedroom for Harry and also served as a kitchen-cum-dining room at meal times. Its bonnet was latched on the front grill. The latch snapped in the strong winds on the coast of the Black Sea and the bonnet opened up like the jaws of a crocodile, completely blocking his front view as he zigzagged all over the road- not knowing where he was going. Harry was a restorer of artwork in old historical buildings, such as famous churches and cathedrals, by profession. His full name was Harrold.M.Kolk. I called him 'Harry' or 'Dutch'. He called me, 'Bali' or 'Hindi'.

So, that was how this strange but remarkable character joined the bandwagon on the borders of

Bulgaria. We were hungry and decided to proceed to Sofia, only some miles ahead.

I was now getting impatient to get to the thick and thin of this venture i.e. the Middle East. My road map showed only one super highway called the 'Autoput' in Yugoslavia, like 'Auto Bahn' in Germany, and 'Motorways' in England. Halting in a Youth Hostel at Graz, I crossed Yugoslavia in a day's drive, and by the evening hit the border of Bulgaria. The only outstanding sight witnessed on the stretch was a head on collision of two large trucks going in opposite directions. How they collided in the middle of the wide lonely road, proved that truck drivers are quite the same the world over, i.e. unyielding in giving way to others.

Sofia was miles away; I intended to stop there for a meal or perhaps for the night.

My VW Beetle and Harry's Citroen

Me and some local Shepherds at Bulgaria

CHAPTER – 3

SCENIC BULGARIA

In Bulgaria, everyone bore a marrow look revealing the oppressive regime, then. We went to a restaurant where we had to stand in a long queue to buy a ticket for the only meal available. At the counter, the meal was impersonally doled out on a plate. There was a couple sitting next to our table- rather a man sitting on a chair and his lady friend sitting on his lap. As he turned around and saw me, he just stood up unceremoniously dropping the lady on the floor. Dragging a chair, he sat next to me and asked if I was an Indian.

He then began narrating the wonderful time he had had in Bombay many years back. To our utter discomfort, he started insisting that we take him with us in the car. On our refusal, he became aggressive and created quite a scene. The police soon arrived and dragged him away leaving us badly shaken.

Harry gave me an excellent idea to spend the night in our respective cars instead of looking for accommodation. Therefore, I unbolted the backrest of the left- hand seat and laid it down in continuation with the backseat. This made a sufficiently long cozy bed with my feet extending underneath the front dashboard. I had brought four very warm blankets and in no time wrapped myself around them. It used to be very cold outside and the moisture breathed out turned into white frost over the windows.

Even the strong frosty winds on the mountains of Turkey made it too cold to bear and often I had to start the heating system in the car. Later, in the deserts of Iraq and Iran, the days were quite warm but the nights were very cold indeed.

Bulgaria was very friendly to India and Holland and we were free to go anywhere. So, we made it a point to go through every road shown in the map. This was the best way to get to know the country. We decided to spend that night at Verna, a lovely holiday resort on the Black Sea.

Verna was a lovely coastal town by the Black Sea. We enjoyed going around. But nobody would talk to us, they just kept mum – I suppose because of the oppressive regime there. Towards the evening we went to a pub, had some grub and some beer. Here the pubs closed very early and abruptly we found ourselves back on the street. If you have a pint or two of beer, nature is bound to call. In a hurry we could not find a toilet. The streets were quite deserted and in a dark alley there was a drain channel. Under the circumstances, Harry and I agreed it would serve our purpose. Just as we were half way through – quite out of the blue, search lights blared at us from different directions, as if we were centre stage in the midst of a performance awaiting applause.

Instead, a couple of fierce looking constables made their presence felt, hauling us unceremoniously and jumped into a waiting police van. As the van started to move, I sensed we were in serious trouble & must do something to stop them from going further. I started shouting at the top of my voice,

'You can't do this to us, we are tourists, we don't know the language, I am an Indian & just won't tolerate it' so on & so forth. Fortunately, one of the guards knew a bit of English and asked me if I was Indian. 'Yes, I Indian, He Dutch.' Bulgaria had very cordial relations, both with India and Holland.

Besides, several theaters were running Raj Kapoor's films which were very popular out there. Perhaps that prompted him to order the driver to stop and let us go. We were most grateful. Unfortunately, we had to toil hard to get back to the place we had started from. We were so disgusted with the whole episode that we went back to the same spot and finished our unfinished symphonies. Oh! What a relief it was!

My Favourite Fish

Harry had planned to go round the Mediterranean and cross over to Gibraltar by boat and finally driving through the continent back to Holland. My pleasure of his company was possibly limited to the Dead Sea. Earlier, Europe was isolated from Turkey by the Bosphorus Sea, and one could only cross the broad river Bosphorus by boat only. But a brand-new bridge was recently built with lights on both sides. Harry and I reached there by late evening and crossed over to Istanbul. The airport was in sight and we decided to spend the night on its edge. In the morning, we walked down a winding road to a delightful bazaar, similar to what we often see in India. Small make-shift shops decorated with colorful tit-bits hanging down, friendly shopkeepers inviting you to see their wares. We located a vendor with a huge round iron plate on which he was frying small fishes . The fish was served on newspaper sprinkled with lemon juice, salt and a bit of vinegar. It was simply delicious & damn cheap. We lost control of how much we ate. I was reminded of my uncle who used to quote couplets in Sanskrit written by Kalidas or someone, which literally meant ***'Some say that Amrit (nectar) can be found with the Gods (Devas) in heaven. Some say it is found on the lips of a young maiden. But I, who has mastered all scriptures, declare, it lies in the pieces of fish dipped in the juice of lemons.'*** The couplets are obviously words of a fish maniac, but under the circumstances they seemed too true.

The moment we crossed the Bosphorus, two radical changes were visible, the people were more thrifty and smarter, so much so that we had to guard our wallets, which were quickly transferred to other safer parts of our torso. The other minor irritant was the absence of seats in the toilets – a constant reminder that we were now in Asia, and we had to get used to a new posture for our daily calls of nature.

We parked our cars at a prominent road junction and climbed up the slope to have a cup of coffee. As we came out of the coffee shop, I happened to glance at my car. I was shocked to find that a huge Turk was carrying my suitcase and quite a few of my belongings on his head and was waiting to cross the very busy road. I made a dash crying for the car. Harry was baffled but followed suit. When I came up to the tall hefty Turk, he ignored me and was still looking for a gap in the traffic to cross to the other side. I found Harry standing by my side with his hands on his hips wondering what I was up to. He then spotted his own suitcase in the luggage on his head; this had an electrifying effect and he started shouting, 'Hey! That's mine! Thief, Thief.' He made such a noise that a crowd collected. I put my left leg between the Turk's feet and pushed him sideways, upsetting his balance and he came down with a thud along with all the baggage on his head. The crowd overpowered him and we took him to the police station, where he was put behind the bars. The formalities at the police station took a lot of our time and we had to look for a place to stay. Unable to find a Youth Hostel, we booked a room in a hotel.

The room was on the third floor and we carried our bags up. I had brought a steel trunk from India, as initially I had gone to England by ship and carrying it in 1967 was no problem. It had come in very handy for it used to fit nicely in the VW front dicky. All the valuable articles were therefore locked in it. It was no doubt rather heavy, so we decided to leave it in the car. Besides we had left the car parked in the hotel compound, where a night watchman was on guard duty.

Next morning, we woke up early and headed for Ankara, 250 miles away. We had hardly gone 20-30 miles when I had a flat front tyre and had to stop.

When I opened the boot, I was shocked to see my trunk was gone. Nicely folded, a couple of shirts and a few other items like paint, pencil, drawing and painting materials etc. were nicely laid out in the dicky. But all other valuables were gone. Obviously, the wicked man had enough time to select what he wanted, though his wicked sense of humor did not desert him. All the same, that deepened my resolve to get out of the country fast, killing my interest in seeing and visiting places of interest. There was no point in going back and reporting the theft to the police station. The chances of getting back my lost items looked out of question. So, we moved ahead.

The road was absolutely straight as if drawn by a giant ruler. After hundred miles or so, hills appeared on the horizon and the road seemed to go right through the hills.

When we arrived at the hills it was getting dark and we pitched camp behind a hillock. Seats in Harry's Citroen were removed and a mighty dinner of 'seekh kababs' with 'naan' bread was brought from Istanbul, which were quite gratifying, and we consumed them half sitting and half lying down. We had to sit in this dining room of ours as it was too cold outside. We then felt for a cup of coffee for warmth. Harry had a small gas cylinder and a pan was put on the gas. We had our first cup and Harry lit the gas for a second helping of coffee when the car began to shake like a pendulum from left to right, as if a strong man was shaking it from the roof sideways. Of course his Citroen had a soft, springy suspension accentuating the movement. It stopped after a few seconds. We threw the strong beam of our torches all around out of the window but could not see anyone. This happened twice. Third time the shaking was a little more violent and our coffee pan was thrown on the floor. We sat melting, but both had the same idea in our heads. It seemed there was a bit of truth when they say that certain places are haunted. Nothing happened for a long time. So I took one of Harry's tyre levers, opened the car door and walked up to my car carefully looking for footprints or pug marks on the sand, but there were none whatsoever. With the strange happenings of the night the mind was somewhat disturbed and sleep was difficult to come by.

When I opened my eyes in the morning, my face was towards the window. I saw a huge face like a tiger glaring at me that sent a chill down the spine. Without batting my eyelids, very slowly I detangled myself from the blankets and moved up the driving seat, while the beast kept growling and showing his canine teeth, with only the glass window between us. Solidly, in my seat the scene came in full perspective. Actually, the beast was a huge dog, and I was surrounded by curious shepherds with a herd of sheep. Some of them were armed and slowly started coming closer looking at me menacingly. Obviously, their intentions were foul. I had no clue how to deal with this situation. In those days, fortunately I used to smoke. Smokers, when in trouble, instinctively search for a cigarette. I opened the glove compartment and took out a packet, lowering my right window glass, offered a cigarette. Two of them jumped for it - that gave me a brilliant idea. I took out another packet and lowering the glass, further threw the packet as far as I could. They all jumped for it like a pack of wolves, giving me enough time to start the engine and roll off full throttle for the highway. I glanced at Harry who was also ready to take off and was relieved to find his path was clear. As I hit the highway, I looked back, they were head over heels, virtually on top of one another, still trying to retrieve the cigarette packets. The scene was no better than what one can see in the mad game English men play called 'RUGBY'.

Another night we were to witness a strange phenomenon. We were parked behind the safety of a small hill. Coming out of the cars after dinner, we filled our lungs with fresh air. A hill beyond suddenly lit up with millions of specks of light. Soon the specks turned into flames curving up and down. Then it seemed as if a large number of men carrying burning torches were running on a path around the hill spirally clockwise from bottom to the top, and finally vanishing at the top of the hill. There was no singing or any noise of any kind, everything happened silently. We were thoroughly shaken. After a long time, it all subsided as if the ghosts had gone back home and called it a day.

The mystery of shaking of the car was solved the very next day, it was due to an earthquake. But the mystery of the ghostly lights remained as such, until recently, some four or five years back I read in the newspaper about the 'Purnagiri lights'. Apparently, an English explorer had to pitch camp on a hill in Uttaranchal, India. In the night, the hill opposite set ablaze full of lights. He wrote about it as 'Purnagiri Lights' in a newspaper, which created quite a stir and became a much discussed topic among the gentry. Anyway, Purnagiri Temple is a full-fledged Purnagiri Devi shrine now. Though I have not read his version of what he saw, it reassured me that it was not a wild dance of ghosts.

CHAPTER – 4

MEDITERRANEAN HOSPITALITY

TURKEY - Ankara to Latakia –

When we started from Ankara, the next place of importance was Adana, some 500 kms away. The two previous incidents of 'car shaking' and 'Escaping from the menacing shepherds' occurred somewhere on this road. We had a night's halt at Adana. I wondered if this place had some connection with a very sweet 'Raga' by the same name in Hindustani music.

Perpetual nights were on the freezing cold mountain ranges of Turkey. Freezing nights had become quite unbearable and we felt the need to spend some time in warmer places. The Mediterranean was not far off, so we turned left heading for a tourist Resort called Latakia.

On the way to Latakia, we stopped at a petrol pump for petrol, and when I went in the cabin for payment, there were three or four rough & hardcore criminal type of characters sitting round the table having drinks. They quizzed me as to where I came from. They forced me to sit and have a drink with them. The liquor they poured turned out white when mixed with water.

It was simply horrible in taste. I just sipped it and slowly poured it on the floor without their knowledge. After two or three helpings I managed to bid them farewell, quickly left the place with Harry and we managed to get to Latakia. On the outskirts, we parked our car to spend the night.

Next morning, we went sightseeing. It was a beautiful place on the Mediterranean. We happened to bump into a travel agent who became friendly and served as a guide. By the evening, he asked if we would like to have dinner with him. We were delighted & he took us to his house. When the dinner was ready, his mother brought the dishes and saw us. She was quite disgusted with our appearance. We had grown long hair and had not shaved since ages. So, she ordered us to go and get our hair cut and shave before she would serve us food. Our expectations of a home cooked meal got a big jolt. But we were too hungry and submitted to this conditional meal. We meekly went to a barber's shop nearby. After a lovely meal of meat curry, naan and rice, his mother also seemed to like us. Her satisfaction of feeding two hungry souls was quite evident. The sumptuous meal served with motherly affection revived our spirits no end.

Mediterranean climate was warmer and we enjoyed one more day before returning to Adana and later to Aleppo. It reminds me of a small place called Daryabad. I belong to Daryabad, some 70 Km from Lucknow, India – the link being Darya Khan, a general in the Khilji's army.

The next stop was Aleppo, some 450 Km from Adana.

Aleppo (Syria) – Comrade Canadian

Shedding the cold syndrome, we were back to Aleppo and the road to Damascus. It is a lovely place. It was quite a modern city in those days with all the amenities one can think of. At a snack joint, they were serving 'falafel', a long cone made of paper-thin chapatti (Rumali Roti) filled with slices of vertically baked leg of lamb, (free of fat) and onions, salad and some sauces – in all a delicious filling creation. We stayed in a Youth Hostel.

Late in the night, I was woken up by a severe headache and found a lot of smoke in the dormitory. Quite a few boys were smoking Marijuana. I created quite a ruckus and they moved to some other place. I spent 2 nights there and those two nights there was no marijuana smoking.

Next morning, I was approached by a tall young Canadian, who asked me if he could join us. His plan was not very clear, but he seemed to be a nice decent fellow. I was now entering a more hostile region and needed a companion. Harry was likely to go round the Mediterranean and then back to Holland. He joined the band wagon. His name is a bit hazy to me (probably Charles James), because I used to call him Kennedy, and I was Hindi for him. He was doing some sociological research.

Whenever he sat in my car, he became my navigator. Because of the absence of milestones those days, itineraries were prepared beforehand with exact miles calculated from maps to know our exact bearings. Our problem was further complicated by the fact that, often the names of places given on the maps were bestowed by the Englishmen, whilst the local name was quite different. For instance, Aleppo is Hahep, Damascus is Damshek, Cairo – Kabira. Keeping a log of the milometer in the car was also essential; also, conversion of miles to Kms – in all, quite a brain raking job he did very well.

My Genius Idea!

Damascus (Syria) To Amman (Jordon)

No matter how hard we tried, we arrived at the Syria /Jordan border quite late in the evening. Completing the formalities took another hour or so. It was the usual practice to exchange our dollars or pounds into local currency at the border itself. In Syria there was a money exchange market at the roadside. We were bone tired, hungry and cold and we were in a hurry to fulfil these needs in Amman, hardly an hour or two's drive ahead. Harry did suggest that we collect some local currency at the border, but I decided to move on. Jordon was also a part sterling area and I did not foresee any difficulty in changing pounds to Dinar in Amman, being the capital of Jordon.

This was a blunder. In Amman, no one would accept pounds or dollars, without which life came to a standstill. Our condition was getting more desperate due to lack of food, warmth and petrol. In the end I decided to go to a police station. They listened to our problem, sympathized with us, and looking at our condition offered us a most welcome cup of tea, which did raise our spirits somewhat. After an hour or so, they politely told us that if we commit a crime they will oblige us with free meal and a bed; failing that they must say goodbye to us.

As we came out of the warm police station, Harry kept on muttering, 'I told you, but you did NOT listen' which further infuriated me no end. As I came and sat in my car, my eyes fell on a large petrol pump in front of us. This gave me an idea. Banking on my luck, I took the car there and asked the pump operator to fill the tank, which he promptly did. The bill came to an equivalent of 6 or 7 shillings. I gave him a pound note (20 shillings) which made him jump. He categorically told us that pounds and dollars are not acceptable and we must pay in Dinar. We explained our inability to do anything else. He could not possibly take back the petrol from the car. After much arguing and telephoning, he had no choice but to return the remaining 13 odd shillings in local currency, which was, under the circumstances, quite a fortune. We then had a hearty meal of seekh kababs and naan bread, followed by a stay in a youth hostel to spend a truly restful night.

Harry and I were not seeing eye to eye, I noticed he had changed a bit and was throwing admiring glances at me for the brilliant bit of ingenuity. Well, all I can say is 'Necessity is the mother of all inventions.' Then onwards, I was accepted as the captain of the team which was far better than arguments and hot tempers in a historic venture like this. It is far more enjoyable all round where trivialities hardly matter.

Posing with his sweetheart- VW- Beetle

CHAPTER – 5

PARTED WITH DUTCH & CANADIAN - JORDAN

On the insistence of James, we paid a visit to Jericho – a historical place on the coast of Dead Sea. Dead Sea got isolated from the Mediterranean and started drying up. In millions of years, the sea level therefore receded to more than 1000 ft below the sea level of the earth. One can see the marks of erosion showing layers marked on the rocks of mountains rising from the sea. There is a cave on the rock where the famous Dead Sea Scrolls were hidden after Christ was crucified. There are steps leading to the cave, where we visited and had the privilege to see the scrolls wrapped up in some kind of cloth which has survived and preserved the scrolls written some 2000 years back.

The evaporation of water from the sea had also changed the ratio of water to salt and thickened. Its density has become very high. A human body just floats and can never drown in the Dead Sea.

The Atmospheric pressure is also very high because of 1000 ft of extra air pressure, that makes it depressing. This, coupled with dampness due to the sea and the heat of the surroundings made the stay quite unpleasant for me. So, I wanted to get out of there fast.

Cruising along the highway in the company of jokers was pleasant going, but not for long. A shimmering silvery band appeared on the horizon far away, which perplexed me. After a fairly long drive, this silver lining turned out to be a first rate obstacle. Across the highway, appeared before us, a river seemed to be full of spate. This was obviously a seasonal river, flowing through a depression in the road. The road continued at the far end. Water in this desert region is always a welcome sight, and we all took off our shoes to wash our feet and enjoyed a splashing for some time. We had no idea when the river would subside and we may be forced to get stranded for days. I sent tall comrade Kennedy on reconnaissance to find out how deep it was. Plomp! Plomp! He walked across it quite comfortably. Coming back, he announced, 'Oh! It's only knee deep.'

Foolishly, we thought we could cross it if we do it carefully. It did not turn out to be easy. Kennedy's 7 feet stature's knees nearly reached my side windows. I stationed Dutch and Kennedy behind to keep pushing the car with all their might while I drove it, till we climbed the other end. Everything was as planned, but nearly a third of the way through, the car started to drift. In fact, it was a dangerous situation. We could end up at some point from where it would become impossible to bring the car back on the road through the sand. For a moment, I panicked. Again, a simple idea saved the situation. I simply opened the door, the water gushed into the car and it sank. The tyres gripped the road, the car lurched forward charging ahead full throttle for a while, covering most of the remaining distance. Then the engine stalled. I quickly jumped out of the car and dried the plugs and the distributor with my handkerchief. Pressing the self-starter button, the warm engine miraculously started again, and we were only a yard or two short of the end of the river, when after much spurting and coughing, it finally stopped. Pushing the car on to the road, the road was used for drying my precious books. I had layered down on the floor, 50 odd large spools of tape filled with finest Indian and western classical music, hidden under the seats.

Thank God, at least we succeeded in crossing the river. This could have forced us to stay in this remote desolate area for maybe a few days, helplessly waiting for the river to subside. The episode was also a discovery that the VW was amphibian, capable of floating, though the exhaust system gets filled with water, and I for one do not recommend its use as a boat.

There was another vital implication. My friend Harry had planned to go round the Mediterranean and back to Europe and finally Holland. Now Kennedy (James) also wanted to accompany him in his car and fly back to Canada from Europe. I was to go to India, through Iraq, Iran; therefore, time had come to part company. It was painful indeed. We had gone through many difficult situations together and grown accustomed to each other. The worst part of the situation was that now onwards I shall be left all alone to cover the desert and was about to enter the worst and most difficult part of this venture. With damp eyes, we bid farewell, hoping some day we meet again. Within a fortnight, the wish was granted and we were destined to see each other's pretty faces again.

CHAPTER – 6

MY LONE JOURNEY IN ROUGH DESERT

Jericho to Iraq

The border of Iraq from Jericho was approximately 180 miles away and the road was a good newly built highway. The map showed an oil pipeline and the road going along it. The map showed four pumping stations. So, I planned to spend the night at the first pumping station after crossing the border.

By the time I reached the border, it was dark and I was running a mild temperature. During the check post formalities, I asked the officer in charge if there were any small hotels nearby where I could get a cup of tea, as I was running a temperature. The officer first laughed and reminded me I was in the middle of the desert and should not expect such luxuries. He then took my passport and asked me to wait in the next room. An hour passed by and I was getting impatient and restless. Every time I enquired with the sentry, I was sternly told to wait, and he refused to disturb his boss. Another sentry entered and sternly told me that the boss wants to see me. I was in no mood to go through another assault session of unnecessary questioning, so I simply told him to tell his boss to return my passport so that I could make a move as I was not feeling well. Without hesitation, he pointed his gun at me ordering me to just obey.

Strange, how your moods melt away into a single mode of self- preservation when a live gun points at you. The boss ordered me to sit next to him, this time in a chair. He pointed to two large pots of tea with small 'damru' shaped glass cups – one for me and the other for himself. In the same tone he blurted out, 'Drink it!'. Drinking the first cup, my normal smile returned and we started to chat. I found he was a fine man and we joked and laughed till the pots were empty. He then came up to the car to see me off. In that mood of bonhomie, as a mark of gratitude, I asked if he would like to have some bananas. He quickly said, 'Oh I like bananas' and without hesitation grabbed the huge bunch of bananas in his both hands. This huge bunch of bananas I had bought, was meant for self - preservation in the desert in case of mishap. My heart sank and my mood dipped to a low. Remembering his gun-toting sentry, my main concern was his mood and not mine; I sank into the car seat and bade him farewell.

Syrian Desert –

I had now entered the 700 mile (1200Km) stretch of hard-core desert on my route. I was all by myself, tossed into this vast ocean of dry, pure white sand. All one could see were moles and dunes of sand stretching from horizon to horizon. No life, no vegetation, not even a blade of grass. Judging the freshness of a piece of food stuff left behind by some traveler long time back, it appeared even the germs find it hard to thrive in the surroundings. The road was very good but was newly built with no milestones and no traffic at all. Driving all day for hundreds of miles, the scene never changed, and it was frightening. Being alone, I must admit it was frightening to the core. Why not stop and recollect myself a bit? No! Stopping could mean perishing. What if the engine would not restart? Though I was capable and equipped to repair minor breakdowns, yet just the thought was a compelling reason to keep moving.

It was humbling to see myself as a tiny insect trying to cross a vast ocean and left entirely to the mercy of elements. Eventually, out of sheer exhaustion, I did stop. Within seconds I dozed off in the seat. When I woke up, I was in a much-relaxed state of mind. I stepped out of the car and touched the sand and was struck by its purity, the stillness and serene calmness, kind of mesmerized me. I was now enjoying its beauty. All my fears and apprehensions simply melted away and I was the lord of all I surveyed. I was now at peace with the serene surroundings and utter silence. The desert was no longer a burden; I now enjoyed this mood and began to sing out aloud.

The map showed my road going parallel to the pipeline. To my horror the pipeline was running under and was not to be seen. There were four pumping stations and my original plan was to stop at the first station and spend the night in safety.

Towards late in the evening, I arrived at the station which had a large circular concrete compound with a small building in the center, with two to three rooms and large glass windows well-lit inside with tube lights. A few trucks were parked haphazardly in the compound facing different directions. I made the mistake of going round it to see what kind of a place it was. Then I stopped the car and walked over to the building, peeping through the glass windows. Through the cubicle, I could clearly see a number of truck drivers having drinks around a table, singing merrily falling down on the floor.

This was clearly not a place to stop and be in the company of a group of drunkards. So, I decided to move and get out of there fast. Sitting in the car again, I went round to find the road coming into or going out of it.

Unfortunately, I couldn't find the road and panic gripped me. More frantic efforts to find the road yielded nothing. The road just seemed to have vanished. Outside it was very cold, but I was sweating like hell. Then I remembered the gentleman who gave me last minute advice on survival in the desert. His first dictum was to sit down and think – don't panic – stay put.

This is exactly what I tried to do. I came out of the car, took a deep breath of fresh air. With the help of my powerful torch, I started looking out for some clues which could lead to the point of my entry or the road. In this powerful light, a telegraph pole showed up. Now I vaguely remembered, sometimes telegraphic poles did surface on the right-hand side, though I was not quite sure. Nonetheless, I brought out my compass which gave only a vague direction. I then resorted to the age- old system of locating the North Pole star. Once north was located on the sky it was not difficult to see that the telegraph poles were heading roughly towards north. Forgetting all else the car was turned to this direction, sticking close to the poles. It was a rough terrain and no road was to be found. The maps showed no other roads in that region. Hanging all hopes on the telegraphic line, I kept moving along it. This went on for no less than 10 long miles (16Kms). All of a sudden, a pair of headlights bounced in front a few hundred yards away. Slowly it was coming towards me. It seemed a heavily loaded truck was coming. After a few minutes it seemed to turn right and suddenly vanished.

I waited and waited but nothing happened. Cautiously, I advanced towards the spot where the lights vanished. The going roughed for a while and with a big bump I seemed to land on a flat surface. In fact, it was the road I have been dying to find for the last so many tense hours.

I also discovered that I had been going roughly in the right direction, but only about 4-5 mts from the road for the last 10 miles. Not going actually on the road, no wonder the going was so rough and bumpy. This was the closest to getting lost in the desert, but the experience was dreadful enough. I wanted to get out of the situation and decided to drive on. As I steadied myself on the road, I analyzed the episode. The main reason for panic was because I was all alone; it was night time and pitch dark. I also discovered the reason why the lights of the truck coming towards me had suddenly vanished. There was a hillock in line with the road and the road went round it. Since the atmosphere there is absolutely dust free, you don't see a beam of light in the air plus there was nothing else to reflect the light as well, and because of the slight elevation, the road was also not visible.

The hillock was large enough to hide my car behind it. I was bone tired, and after getting a hearty grub, went into the bed. The grub consisted of bread spread with butter and some mango pickle brought in bulk. I still had 3-4 tins of fish but was being saved for future use. All the 'seekh Kababs' bought at Amman had already been consumed in the last few days.

I was now going through the heart of desert track. There were no lush green meadows, with trees laid down with flowers spreading their fragrance, enough to lure Radha & Krishna to materialize in the misty moonlit night by the river Yamuna flowing leisurely yet surging to touch their feet – the kind of imagination several poets like Meera, Surdas, Haridas or Ratnakar created. These were quite out of place, here the sand laden with more sand was spreading from horizon to horizon. Several nights and days had gone by without meeting a single living being. Conditions were really harsh, dreary and frightening, at the same time extremely troubling.

The experience was unique for me and valuable in its own way. It created a strange sense of detachment with the surroundings, which I knew, would undoubtedly be of no use in times of need. Here the mood and the feeling was the one that

Kabir's poetries create – a dreary, dry, down to earth, harsh, 'Nirgun' (without any attributes), 'Nirakar' (without any shape) kind of reality.

Strange, how the surroundings play havoc with your everyday needs. We all know how the feet sink in the sand and the daily chores become a big inconvenience. One day, I came across a couple of abandoned concrete pipes, lying end to end beside the highway. They were the exact distance apart that is about two inches away. Since I had not met a single soul in the last many days; to think of privacy just did not matter. So, there I was, sitting merrily on the pipes easing myself. All these days, I had been pining to meet someone to talk to, and providence did fulfill this wish, for I heard shouts of 'Bravo! Bravo!', as a car-load of boys and girls whizzed past in front of me, and my face must have gone red with embarrassment. How my wish was fulfilled at the most inopportune moment.

Since I used to sleep in the car, it was my home and I had kerosene stove to cook food or make tea or coffee. The food consisted of bread - butter, cheese and tinned fish and meat and mango pickle-which came in handy when I used to run out of tinned stuff. That time, it was just bread and mango pickle. Of course, 'seekh kababs' were commonly available on the roadside but only in towns and cities. In those days, soup packets were not available, but for tinned soup, I had a fair stock. To carry cooked meals needed much effort and was rarely done. There was always a great longing for home cooked meals. Even if somebody out of courtesy invited me for a meal, the chance was always grabbed.

The whole experience of living a nomadic life was a tremendous experience in itself. Fortunately, I never fell ill and my Volkswagen never gave me any trouble that I could not sort out.

Driving along and approaching a town called Rutbah, I noticed a tiny spot on the horizon in front of me. In a few hours of driving, it started to grow red in color. I was intrigued and the desire to know what it was became quite unbearable. Many- many miles later it became large enough to recognize that it was merely a Coca Cola sign mounted on a huge steel structure. This quenched the curiosity but what an idiotic way to advertise, as from now onwards a most vicious obsession to have a coke was simply torturous. My mental state dipped to breaking point. Many miles later, a booth appeared in a small settlement where the thirst for Cola was finally quenched. The monotony and loneliness in the desert, and sometimes the heat during the day can easily turn into full-fledged mental distortions one should guard against.

Mirage is another mind- boggling reality in these regions. You can clearly see a village like habitat near the horizon with date trees growing beside a shimmering pool of water, the womenfolk carrying pitchers on their heads, children playing, animals grazing, etc. As you keep going towards it, yet you never seem to reach there. The image of this scene in fact goes through an optical process called refraction, through rarified layers of hot air, warmed by the sand absorbing heat from the sun. The image metaphors several times, as the distance incurred many - many miles away. This way you see what is happening maybe hundreds of miles away.

CHAPTER – 7

WELCOME REUNION WITH MY PALS - IRAQ

It was highly relieving to see some vegetation and population after the desert stretch. I was now entering the borders of Iraq. At the check post, I was just wondering why the inspector was viewing my passport with great interest, when he informed me that two persons were searching for me. For an instant, I was perplexed as to whom they might be. I had a friend in Baghdad with whom I had planned to stay, but he won't try to collect me from the Iraq border. I was so tired I couldn't think much, so I decided to search for the nearest Youth Hostel and get myself some rest and good food, before starting for Baghdad.

The Youth Hostel Receptionist was pleased to hear my name and for the second time I was told that two persons were searching for me. I was bewildered. The experience of driving through the desert alone had already exhausted me to the point of madness, and I just wanted to eat and rest, I couldn't afford to deal with suspense now. Suddenly I found myself asking the receptionist, 'Did they tell their names?' And the reply I got lifted my spirits no end, he said 'Ya, I wrote, here...er... Mr. Harrold and Mr. James. They asked for you to wait for them, if they are not here.'

Lo & Behold! I turned and saw my dear friends again and ready to accompany me for the rest of my trip to India. After parting from me they had met with an accident and Harry's car had to be deserted. Luckily, they were not hurt. Soon they realized that they wanted to accompany me rather than go back home. They were curious about seeing India too. I was glad we were together again, though after crossing the most difficult part of the journey alone.

I was also used to their company and going alone was a bit of a burden on my mind which was released now. I got a good night's sleep that day.

I had an old friend Jaffar to meet in Baghdad, and he was waiting eagerly for me. In the excitement of meeting him and enjoying his wife's hospitality, time just slipped away, and I did not realize that I had a visa for only one week. I had overstayed for about a week. On reaching Iraq / Iran border, several tourists told me it was a serious negligence on my part. First of all, the Border post In-charge would definitely send me back to Baghdad for a fresh visa, which in normal circumstances, can be made at the border. Because of politically volatile situation in the country, and having failed to report to the police, I may have to do a lot of explaining. That had really scared me, for that would mean going back hundreds of miles and then coming back, plus all the rigorous hassles of getting a new visa.

So, as I entered the cabin of the check-Post, I sincerely prayed to God to get me out of this sticky situation. It seemed the line was free and he heard my feeble voice. And then, something of a benevolent best, just sort of a mini- miracle happened. Just as I handed over my passport to the officer, the lights suddenly went out. This was a very unusual thing to happen in those areas. There was a wild scramble for a torch and a candle. Finally in the dim candle-light, he failed to notice the expiry date, and with a loud swear (in Arabic) banged my passport with the seal of approval. Promptly, I grabbed the passport from his hands, slipped out to collect my wits and gave heartful thanks to him.

Tehran –

It was evening when we reached Tehran, a most modern city and as neat and clean as any European city. We found accommodation in a Youth Hostel. Our first shock came when we learnt that we would be forced to stay in this hostel for the next 7 days, reason being that the Shah of Iran had been blessed with a son and a week's complete holiday had been declared. No issue of visas or any business with banks etc.

Now we heard a shriek from Harry. He had an encounter with a live mosquito, which he had never seen before in his life, and it frightened him to no end. We closed the doors and one by one eliminated all the mosquitoes we could lay our hands on by throwing a pillow at them, wherever it landed.

A week's time was ample to see all the sights worth seeing. I was keen on seeing the 'Peacock Throne'. It was the most beautiful piece – a golden throne studded with precious jewels in the most artistic image of a peacock. A peacock design is undoubtedly the most elegant and priceless piece of art.

Tehran to Mashhad -

We were going smoothly towards a road a few miles away, running parallel to the rim of the Caspian Sea. Abruptly, the road turned into the most torturous and bumpy road I had ever come across. It was like a corrugated sheet, with 5-6” deep crusts and troughs about 6-7” apart. One can well imagine how bone shaking it would be. The worst part was that it went on and on, like a reversed speed breaker for no less than a few hundred miles, which took more than a couple of days to cross. The experience was shaking and absolutely maddening, leaving us thoroughly rattled and jittery. Apparently, the road was damaged and left in this condition by the movement of hundreds of tanks that went over the road during the Second World War.

Eventually, the tie rod of the front wheel of my car was damaged, ruining the front wheel alignment; as a result, the front wheel wobbled left and right between 3-5”. I was shocked to see that within these 500 miles, the front wheel tyres were worn out. Finally, I managed to acquire a new tie rod that was available only in the VW Service Station at Kabul, which completely cured the wobbling problem.

The Beautiful Mosque of Mashhad -

Mashhad was another memorable little place on my route that is still stuck in my memory. The entire population and township surrounds a large beautiful mosque on top of a hill, dominating the whole scenery. When we took a close view of the mosque, it was so captivating that the desire to enter and see the inside was irresistible. People had warned us that we should never disturb the religious sentiments in these regions, as someone may over-react and you could end up getting your throat slit. We dared not enter it.

As Harry and Kennedy would attract attention as tourists; they threw a challenge at me, that I dare enter it. It was prayer time and the entrance was crowded. Risking my neck, I slipped into the mosque, and am glad I did. It was a delight to see the beautiful jaded carvings under the dome in soothing shades of light blue and green on the white background, repeated green and white marble on the minarets. The courtyard had a matching checkered floor of finely chiseled floral designs. The pattern reminds us of how the artists and artisans had poured all their religious fervor in such a refined and cultured manner for Allah, the almighty and benevolent, who I am sure, must be mighty pleased and showered his benevolence on them.

The side galleries on the four sides of the courtyard were filled with cut-glass décor and superb chandeliers hanging from the roof. I was over-awed with the splendor, looking around with an open mouth.

As I slipped out of the magnificent mosque of Mashhad, Harry and Kennedy were eagerly waiting for me to describe my experience. I narrated as best as I could about what I saw inside. They heard the whole story with great attention. In the end I muttered, 'I wish you had seen it too.' They reacted in their own way, but the message was the same, 'Well ! If you have seen it, we all have seen it.' This touching remark strengthened the bond of comradery and togetherness between us.

From the high pedestal of the mosque, we came down to the township around it. The streets and the bazaars were similar to what we see in India. For Harry and Kennedy, it was quite exciting. As we were hungry, we came up to a roadside joint where meat curry and seekh kababs were available. There, I spotted a huge 4 ft long, fish shaped thick sheets hanging by hooks. Out of curiosity, I enquired what they were. I was quite shocked to know that they were 4ft long naans, that is bread. It was good in taste and very cheap. Being an engineer, I was curious to know how such a huge naan was made and baked. The shopkeeper took me to the oven which looked more like boilers. In the middle, there was a horizontal tray of steel net carrying red hot embers of coal and a bed of round pebbles down below on the floor. The bread dough was kneaded and spread in the shape of a 4ft long naan, then scooped into a tray with a handle and thrown on the stone bed. In a few minutes the brown naan was ready for us.

The main problem encountered now was the absence of any milestones, which were not installed on the roads as yet. Though the newly built roads were excellent, but we did not know where we were. We happened to find a family having a picnic beside the road on the lush green grass verge. So, we stopped to ask how far the next post of call was. They were educated and well to do people and invited us to join them. They were pleased to know that I was Indian and my friend Dutch. We had a few snacks and had a pleasant time. We were getting ready to leave when an elderly lady asked through the father, what my name was. I got the hint, yet I obliged. Now they wanted to know if I was Hindu, to which I nodded. There was a wild commotion. They all stood up muttering, 'Kafir! Kafir!' and some of them even spit on the ground. We first got up, bowed and thanked them for their hospitality and quickly made for the car. If you opt for a trip like this, one should expect all *shades of hospitality*. Trying our best to get this sour experience out of our minds, we drove off full throttle.

A little blunder - Kabul via Kandahar –

We had a hearty meal and hung a piece of naan between the front and the back seats.

Now it was time to plan the final assault to India through Afghanistan. From Mashhad, the shorter route of 1350Kms drive on a fairly good road, amid mountainous regions to Kabul through Herat – Farah and Kandahar. As per our pact made in Baghdad, when all three joined, that if I am unable to get a visa for Pakistan, I shall fly over Pakistan to Amritsar, and Harry and Kennedy will drive the car through Pakistan to join me in Amritsar. Time had come to implement it as the visa was not granted to me.

Too much driving had taken a toll on me. I had therefore handed over complete charge of navigation to Kennedy, who did it very well. As almost all the highways in the middle-east at that time were brand new and no mile- stones or directions of any kind were there. There was no traffic also, or human beings in sight to help us. Therefore, our day's itinerary had to be carefully worked out i.e. distances accurately noted from maps and listed, and the miles converted on the milometer on the car, accurately logged.

Mashhad to Kabul highway bifurcated at Kandahar – One straight to Kabul and the other went to Pakistan. I had instructed Kennedy to be very careful at Kandahar and put us on the correct road. He had become quite proficient in navigation, but this time he created a massive blunder. After driving about 160 Kms, suddenly soldiers started popping out of the sand, ready to challenge us. They had Pakistani markings on their uniforms; I made a fast U-turn back to Kandahar.

This little blunder cost us a 300Km round trip at a time when we were getting impatient to reach India.

Kandahar to Kabul –

Now that we were sure that we were on the correct road to Kabul; we were in a relaxed mood and the going was good. The scenery was changing, leaving behind the sand and the desert; we were climbing rocky mountainous and windy roads. For the first time in my life, I was witnessing plateau-like formations of the mountains.

As we went on, there were other noticeable features too, like, though the sand had vanished and we were going light, but it was equally desolate. The mountains were slabs of rocks, as if layered one on top of the other, but completely devoid of vegetation of any kind. No plants, trees or flowers. Absence of moisture in the air failed to encourage the growth of moss – often found in the Himalayas, when you go beyond the tree-line.

Kandahar to Kabul was some 200 Kms and we reached there in the afternoon. Kabul is located on the top of a hill on a good flat piece of ground, criss -crossed with streams flowing at places. It had the much welcome greenery. I had my cousin Gopal ji, who was working in an Embassy. Gopal ji was his nickname when we were young, that I knew, but the name he was using now was Rajendra Bali; his real name. This created some difficulty in locating him. Anyways, we finally found him and had a wonderful stay with him. We had an excellent sight -seeing tour of Kabul. The part that Harry and Kennedy enjoyed most was a spritely horse-driven tonga ride around the city.

CHAPTER – 8

TRAIL OF MY FATE

Now was the time to make the final entry to India. But the road was going through Pakistan and I failed to get a Transit Visa through Pakistan. Dutch and Canadian had no problem getting a transit visa. There were also no import restrictions, so they could take the car through Pakistan. So, it was decided that they will drive my car through Pakistan, and I will take a flight from Kabul to Amritsar and finally meet them at the border the next morning at about 10 a.m. As I had mentioned earlier, I had a document for the car known as ' carnet de passage de Douanes.' This was meant to by-pass any important formalities - such as duty etc. in the countries mentioned in the Carnet. As I entered a country, an entry was registered and on exit, the Carnet was discharged from that country. When I had entered Afghanistan, the car was entered, but I did not know how to get it discharged when the car left the country. So, I did the wisest thing of the whole trip, which will soon be clear. I took the pain of going up to the Afghan/Pakistan border at Khyber-pass and get the Carnet discharged and somehow managed to slip back to the bus stop.

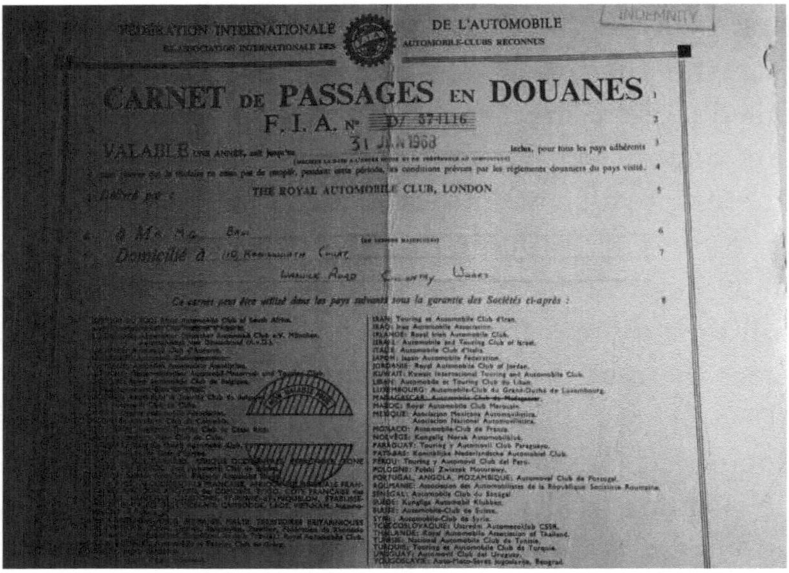

INDEMNITY

FÉDÉRATION INTERNATIONALE DE L'AUTOMOBILE

ET ASSOCIATION INTERNATIONALE DES AUTOMOBILE-CLUBS RECONNUS

CARNET DE PASSAGES EN DOUANES

F. I. A. Nº D/ 371116

VALABLE une année, soit jusqu'au 31 JAN 1968 inclus, pour tous les pays adhérents

Délivré par : THE ROYAL AUTOMOBILE CLUB, LONDON

Ce carnet peut être utilisé dans les pays suivants sous la garantie des Sociétés ci-après :

Carnet de passage de Douanes

Again, luck did not favor me fully. Because of the dangerous terrain, traffic was completely stopped as soon as the sun set. Therefore, the last bus for Kabul left at 12'o clock and I missed it. Khyber-pass was a remote area with only one border post and of course a bus stop. I had no idea where to park myself for the night and badly missed my chariot cum home, my lovely Beetle. I was lucky to meet a Pakistani gentleman who readily put me up for the night in his house and I realized that there were hardly any houses in the small settlement. He was also kind enough to offer me dinner which was a good hearty meal. Next morning, I took the first bus to Kabul so that I could catch my flight to Amritsar.

I had cleared all formalities with the Customs, and was sitting in my seat on the plane when there was a re-checking of the passports. I had the entry relating to my car on the passport. I was detained at the Airport.

Next morning, I approached the Counsel of Imports & Exports. At first, he was adamant. He wanted me to get back the car first, before proceeding with the matter. Fortunately, someone sitting next to him fired the question at me asking if I have any proof that the car had left Afghanistan? I showed him the 'Discharged Cornet'. He at once pronounced that since the car had already left the country, of which I had a valid proof with me; I do not come under the purview of Export-Import Regulations, or any liability to pay any duty etc. Therefore, I should be allowed to go out of the country. Reluctantly, I was granted permission, but I missed my flight again.

Unfortunately, the flights were bi-weekly, and the next flight was two days later. I wondered what Harry and Kennedy would do, not finding me at the border. There was no means to communicate with them. I just prayed they would stay put till I arrived.

Finally, I landed on my homeland at Amritsar, India two days later. By the time I reached Ferozpur Border (called Hussainiwala in Pakistan) from Amritsar, I was more than a week late. By then Harry and Kennedy had panicked and went back all the way to Karachi (500 Kms) to their embassies. Harry was advised to go back and try again. I waited another couple of days, having no clue of their whereabouts.

In those days, we could see past the borders, I could see Pakistan Check post from the Indian border, then the barricading and a passage of no-man's land, till the beginning of the Indian border.

By mid-day on the third day, as I was standing discussing my matter with a security personnel, I heard loud shrieks of "Bali...Bali". I couldn't believe the sight of Harry running like a child would on finding his mommy after a long time. In the excitement of sighting me, he forgot all about the perilous borders he was walking on. With his hands raised up in the sky, he kept running. He had almost stepped on the no-man's land, when several guns pointed at him, and a guard shouted "Savdhaan" (meaning alert). Poor Harry didn't know what it meant but realized immediately that he might get shot if he didn't stop. Next moment he just froze, one leg in the air and both hands pointing at the sky. Even in danger, it was a pose worth capturing.

He spent some time explaining about his deranged state of mind owing to the long drive and some unforeseen circumstances. After about an hour's time they finally got through and the car was officially imported into India with no further hassles.

At every stage, we seemed to run into difficulties, but as the saying goes, 'All is well that ends well'.

India – Amritsar to Delhi

Now that we were on Indian soil, we set our course towards Delhi.

The weather was reasonably hot in April. I remember spotting sugarcane juice vendors by the roadside. We were tempted to try it. I had just one glass but Harry and Kennedy loved it so much that they gulped down 4 or 5 large glasses. Their stomachs could not hold the stuff, and I had to stop the car every 15 minutes by their shouts, 'Stop! Stop! I can't hold it!' That is how they left their mark throughout the Amritsar- Delhi highway; considerably slowing down our progress.

By the time we reached Delhi, it was quite late in the evening. It took us another hour to locate my brother Kaushlendra's house in Defence colony.

We terrified him by arriving in the middle of the night, grabbed things to eat and slept on whatever we could find. After resting, the next day, we proceeded towards Daryabad near Lucknow, where my mother was desperately waiting for me.

Daryabad – The final Destination –

My mother, who was living with my eldest brother's family, was quite ill and extremely worried. She had no idea about my well-being since the past two months. In those times, tele communication was confined to a few lucky people, and to my surprise all my post-cards and letters, which I posted from various places on my trip, never reached her.

I knew her greatest fear was that I would land up unannounced, with a female of foreign origin by my side, and take her to her wits.

In utter excitement to reach home and for the purpose of surprising my mom a bit more, I told her, 'Don't be mad, a female has come with me.'

Without showing much of her emotions, her eyes expressed her curiosity. I took her outside in the porch, and introduced her to my Sweetheart (as I called her)- My sweet little Volkswagen Beetle! My mother couldn't help laughing, and the proud, happy and content gleam her eyes portrayed at that moment, continue to sparkle my eyes even today.

Later, even as a 31year old youth, I could not help lying down beside her. She sat up and put my head in her lap. The aura of love and affection, her lovelorn hands caressing my head did, was something only a mother can do. It reassured me that I had reached HOME. The kind of peace, security and contentment that descended upon me in her lap, they say, is even God's envy.

Methodist House, where he lived and made friends from various continents.

Playing Cricket on the streets of Coventry, England

Picture from a local newspaper, playing Chess

With his wife, Mrs. VijayBala Bali

The sound system he created for his tape recorder that matched the Dolby sound system of today.